Gore Vidal

The
American
Presidency

Odonian Press
distributed through
Common Courage Press / LPC Group

Additional copies of this and other Odonian Press Real Story books are available at most good bookstores, or directly from Common Courage Press. For a list of other titles, and details on ordering, see the inside back cover. To order by credit card, or for information on quantity discounts, please:

- call 207 525 0900 or 800 497 3207
- fax 207 525 3068
- email *odonian@realstory.com*
- visit the Odonian website at *www.realstory.com*
- write Common Courage at Box 702, Monroe ME 04951

Distribution to the book trade is through LPC Group, 1436 W. Randolph St, Chicago IL 60607. To order, call 800 243 0138. Real Story books are also available through wholesalers.

Data entry: **Chad Lehrman, Jim Bier** *(Tucson)*

Compilation: **Arthur Naiman, Jim Bier**

Editing: **Arthur Naiman**

Picture research: **Erfert Fenton** *(San Jose CA)*

Illustrations of presidents: **InterComm** *(Los Angeles)*

Photograph on page 88: **Larry Powell** *(Asheville NC)*

Design and layout: **Arthur Naiman**

Copyediting & proofreading: **Susan McCallister** *(Berkeley CA)*

Index: **Ty Koontz** *(Boulder CO)*

Logistics: **Richard Korol** *(Tucson)*

Emotional triage: **Meg St. John**

Intuitnet access: **Janee Campagne** *(Tucson)*

Copyright © 1996–98 by Gore Vidal. All rights reserved, including the right to reproduce or copy this book, or any portions of it, in any manner whatever (except for excerpts in reviews).

Printed in the USA   First printing—August, 1998

Library of Congress catalog card number: 98-30178

**An Odonian Press Real Story book
published through Common Courage Press / LPC Group**

Odonian Press gets its name from Ursula Le Guin's wonderful novel *The Dispossessed* (though we have no connection with Ms. Le Guin or any of her publishers). The last story in her collection *The Wind's Twelve Quarters* also features the Odonians (and Odo herself).

Odonian Press donates at least 10% of its aftertax income to organizations working for social justice.

TABLE OF CONTENTS

GORE VIDAL ❧ THE AMERICAN PRESIDENCY

EDITOR'S NOTE

This book began as three half-hour programs on British television; to those scripts
Gore Vidal added almost 50% more new
material. After I compiled everything, he
made final corrections and changes.

Arthur Naiman

ABOUT THE AUTHOR

The grandson of Thomas Pryor Gore, the
populist senator from Oklahoma, Gore Vidal
was born October 3, 1925 at West Point,
where his father was aeronautics instructor
and football coach. He wrote his first novel
at the age of 19, while he was in the army,
and was widely hailed as a boy genius.

Since then he's written dozens of novels—
*Burr, 1876, Julian, Creation, Myra Breck-
inridge* and *Myron* among them—countless
essays and reviews, plays, screenplays, tele-
plays, short stories and a fascinating memoir, *Palimpsest.* Many of his novels have
been number-one bestsellers, and collec-
tions of his essays have won both the
National Book Award and the National Book
Critics Circle Award.

As a reviewer in the *Washington Post* put
it, "I can't think of another author more
certain to have exactly the right opinion on
absolutely everything."

I think it might prove interesting, as century and millennium end, to take a brief look at the American presidency. Yes, I know that, for most Americans, the presidents are just so many interchangeable faces on the money, now in such short supply for so many.

Even so, our presidents, often working as if from a master plan, were able to achieve in a little over two centuries the first global empire. So let us contemplate a sort of success story.

Currently, the American empire is governed not from the Oval Office but from the White House TV studio, from which His Imperial Majesty is beamed into every home and heart this side of the elusive and perhaps subversive Internet. But the president is still military master of our planet and its dull moon.

TV politics

In a sense, our latest batch of presidents is above politics. A president is elected to a four-year term, while his campaign for election also lasts four years. He who can raise the most money to buy time on television is apt to be elected president by that less than half of the electorate which bothers to vote.

Since the same corporations pay for our two-party, one-party system, there is little or no actual politics in these elections. But we do get a lot of sex. Also, he who subtly hates blacks the most will always win a plurality of the lily-white hearted.

The word *liberal* has been totally demonized, while *conservative*—the condition of most income-challenged Americans—is being tarnished by godly pressure groups whose symbols are the fetus and the flag. As a result, today's candidates rush toward a meaningless place called "the center," and he who can get to the center of the center—the dead center, as it were—will have a four-year lease on the White House TV studio.

Paradoxically, he will have almost no power within the country. Economic affairs are decided by the corporate ownership of the country and their Congress. Recently, Mr. Clinton felt obliged to remind the other TV luminaries that, at least under the Constitution, the president is not—repeat *not*—irrelevant at home.

But in foreign affairs he is preeminent, and it has been our presidents, since 1800, who have kept us perpetually on the move and—more often than not—at war, so that today we have military bases in every corner of the earth. Unfortunately, there is now no money to pay for them and no evil empire ritually to confront.

But that's the end of the story. Let's start at the beginning.

American exceptionalism

We were the exception to the old laws of European history. We had more land than we needed. Our presidents were simply men of property elected to preside over thirteen states that looked after themselves. But, as we shall see, this virtuous and unique American exceptionalism didn't last very long.

The wars in Europe between England and France were reflected—crucially—in America. The French, in alliance with the native Mongols, fancifully called Indians, fought against the English.

Since the government in London protected the colonies, it expected to be paid for its services. So it taxed the colonists. When the French wars ended, it went right on taxing them. When there were protests,

Westminster sent out royal governors who dissolved assemblies and increased taxes.

Officially, this was the reason for the so-called American revolution. "No taxation without representation" was the cry. But the actual reason for the split was geographical. No small island, no matter how prettily sceptered, can govern from three thousand miles away three million people scattered across 473,000 square miles.

The Declaration of Independence

Inspired by the Enlightenment of the 18th century, not to mention Rousseau's "noble savage," we created ourselves. This act of creation was principally the work of Thomas Jefferson, a Virginia planter of many talents who would later become our third president.

On July 4, 1776, Jefferson launched the Declaration of Independence, the most important document in American history, describing why the thirteen colonial states of America must now break away from irrelevant British rule—not to mention taxes. "All men are created equal and independent," it declared in its original draft. And "from that equal creation they derive rights inherent and inalienable, among which are the preservation of life, and liberty, and the pursuit of happiness."

Thomas Jefferson, 1801–1809

"Life" and "liberty" are cherished old friends when it comes to political rhetoric, as they always make a nice contrast to death and slavery, two conditions most human beings would rather avoid. But the pursuit of happiness was a new notion—for a new nation, or for anyone.

It is, of course, suitably vague. But the idea that the state exists only to promote

9

the welfare—and happiness—of the citizens that comprise it was a total break from the hierarchic class system of old Europe, where the populace were as so many bees to serve the sovereign in her hive.

Jefferson was not so much the founder of the American political system—no one could be so cruel as to ascribe that to him—as he was the inventor of the American Idea, which reminded the world of American exceptionalism. Jefferson's own dream was a sort of vague—always vague—Arcadia, home to independent farmers. He embodied the Southern ideal: less government is best.

His enemy, Alexander Hamilton of New York, preferred cities to farms, international trade to self-sufficiency. The division between Jefferson and Hamilton was at the heart of our system from the beginning and continues, in decadent form, to this day.

Hamilton's system led eventually to industrialization, foreign wars and great wealth for the few. Jefferson's system led, finally, to civil war, as his agrarian Arcadia was founded upon the peculiar institution of slavery.

Jefferson declared all men to be created equal. But then he had to make an exception for African slaves on the ground that they weren't, properly speaking, people. He himself owned as many as 200 slaves at one point, some of them his own half-breed children.

On a series of often dramatic contradictions, a nation was conceived. Happily, in the 19th century, Ralph Waldo Emerson cut the Gordian knot of perpetual contradiction when he told us most loftily, "With consistency, a great soul has simply nothing to do." Everyone was greatly relieved.

The Declaration of Independence was not just a hymn to liberty—it was a call to arms, read to inspire troops under the command of the British-trained general from Virginia, George Washington. Though Washington never actually won a proper battle, he had a strong and persistent character. He muddled through to victory, thanks to the support of the French and to the fact that his British opposite, Cornwallis, was no Napoleon either.

The Constitutional Convention

The victorious colonies had now become the United States of America. Well, not so very united. In 1786, when a group of ex-soldiers realized that they were paying more tax to the Massachusetts government than they had ever paid to the British, they went into brief rebellion under one Daniel Shays. During the ensuing panic, Washington and the rest of the landowning class realized that without a strong central government, their landholdings were at risk.

In the spring of 1787, an emergency convention was held in Philadelphia. Its purpose was to design a government that would, above all, protect the rights of property. In the process, the peculiar notion of the American presidency was born.

Jefferson, at a safe remove in Paris, where he was American minister, hailed the delegates as "an assembly of demigods." He also had his own man, James Madison, in place to make sure that we could never become a monarchy or a democracy. What was wanted—and achieved—was the best sort of government for white Anglo-Saxon Protestant men of property to do business in.

As President Coolidge put it much later, in the 1920s: "The chief business of the American people is business." By the 1950s, President Eisenhower's secretary of defense, Charles Wilson, announced: "What is good for General Motors is good for America." He had been the president of General Motors, of course.

Business was to run the presidency until...but let's not spoil the suspense.

James Madison, 1809–1817

Back at the convention, the office of president was carefully hedged round—as were
the people at large—with all sorts of
Venetian-style checks and balances.
Madison, among others, was quite aware
that ambitious presidents would be tempted
to prosecute wars. So the power to declare
war was reserved to Congress. Then, to
make doubly sure, the power of the purse

was also reserved to Congress. If the president wanted adventures, he'd have to beg.

Then, somewhat absent-mindedly, gazing at the dignified presiding officer of the convention, General Washington, they made the president commander-in-chief of the armed forces and decided that foreign affairs would be pretty much his business. Thus the bright brazen thread of tyranny was woven into the respectable flannel of a virtuous mercantile republic.

Mischief is now afoot.

The delegates knew that Washington was bound to be our first president, despite his usual "I'm not worthy" protestations, so they tailored the office to fit his majestic presence. He had fought for the British against the French—and had been defeated at what is now Pittsburgh.

He was abnormally tall, a talented surveyor, and, famously, had wooden teeth. He had acquired much of his fortune in the most honest way—he had married it. The first president was our first millionaire.

He did not disappoint. Washington presided over economic recovery and he added the states of Vermont, Kentucky and Tennessee to the Union, thus beginning the inexorable move to the west, an expansion which would become more and

George Washington, 1789–1797

more continental as it became less and less constitutional.

John Adams, one of the most brilliant and eccentric of the founders, thought the whole business lacked magic. Too much gray flannel. He hated the title of *president.* "Fire brigades and cricket clubs have presidents," he wrote. "He will be despised to all eternity. 'His Most Benign Highness' is the correct title."

Adams was to be our first vice president and second president. He was known to his amused contemporaries as His Rotundity, for obvious reasons.

John Adams, 1797–1801

The Bill of Rights

Most of the Constitution-makers took a dim view of their creation. Few thought that it could—or should—last. Jefferson suggested a total overhaul once a generation.

As it was, at the last minute, ten amend-ments were attached to the Constitution. They ensured freedom of speech, of assem-bly, due process of law, and so on. These amendments are known as the Bill of Rights and they are the second great innovation, as well as lawful proof of our exceptionalism.

No other society had ever thought up anything so breathtakingly simple. As a result, the great dominations and powers of the country have been devoted ever since to ridding the people at large of these unseemly protections.

The Louisiana Purchase

Oddly enough, it was our third president, Thomas Jefferson, the believer in minimal government, a modest presidency and a demure, mind-your-own-business repub-lic, who first burst out of the confines of the Constitution.

When Napoleon Bonaparte conquered Spain, he took over the Spanish colonies in North America. He was also faced with a highly expensive slave rebellion in Haiti which frightened Jefferson—so near to home—and bored Napoleon, who was only interested in conquering as much of Europe as possible. But that cost money, so Napoleon offered to sell the stolen Spanish lands to the United States for $27,267,000.

Jefferson leapt at the deal, though he had no right to act on his own. He purchased what was called Louisiana—885,000 square miles, from the Mississippi to the Rockies, from the Gulf of Mexico to Canada, acquiring in the process the crucial port city of New Orleans, whose Catholic Creole inhabitants' pursuit of happiness was stopped dead in its tracks.

Jefferson had now set an example for later presidents to act unilaterally and the stuff of the Constitution is beginning to come unraveled.

The westward course of empire

By the 1830s, a new generation had come to power. Jefferson's rather nervous land deal had made a great impression, particularly on Tennessee's Andrew Jackson. Old Hickory, as he was called, was the first of the new breed of deliberate expansionists. Son of Ulster immigrants, he was a successful general, planter, duelist and Indian killer.

Andrew Jackson, 1829–1837

He was the people's president to such an extent that those who supported him called themselves the Democratic Party. He even invited "the people" to the White House on the day of his inauguration. They wrecked the place, and he had to spend his first night as president in a hotel. Personally, he never much liked the folks.

During his two terms, Jackson broke 93 treaties with the Indian tribes. White men wanted Indian land. And Indians were only savages, weren't they? But the Cherokee nation had a written language in which they published books and newspapers; they also established schools and businesses.

Jackson was ruthless—and a figure for his successors to emulate. Under the Removal Act, the Indians were driven west across the Mississippi River. Many thousands died along the Natchez Trace, known to the Indians to this day as the Trail of Tears. (A few years later, the Gore family acquired most of the Chickasaw territory in northern Mississippi and started its own rustic regional dynasty.)

The most blatant of our expansionists was our eleventh president, James Knox Polk. An intelligent, low-key figure, he prepared the annexation of Texas. He was able to peacefully draw the boundary between the United States and Canada, which gave us Oregon. Then, he looked south and was ravished by what he saw.

"We must have California," Polk said, and offered the Mexicans a derisive sum for it. It was refused, so he resorted to other means. On May 13, 1846, the United States declared war on Mexico.

James Polk, 1845–1849

General Ulysses S. Grant, a future president, later wrote that it was one of the most unjust wars ever waged by a stronger against a weaker nation. He believed that our Civil War was divine punishment for this transgression.

Polk defeated Mexico and we got California, where gold was soon discovered. America was to be rich, and the dreams of our expansionist presidents had been fulfilled. The nation now spanned the continent.

Ulysses S. Grant, 1869–1877

Lincoln

What next? Abraham Lincoln was next, and the secession of the slave states and civil war. Suddenly our continental nation was falling apart.

Lincoln was easily the most brilliant and mysterious of our presidents. Though he did not want to abolish slavery, he did warn that a house divided against itself cannot stand, much less a nation half slave, half free. He himself simply stood for the Union forever.

Abraham Lincoln, 1861–1865

The Southern states said that if the nominee of the new Republican Party, Lincoln, was elected president, they would go. He was elected—barely—and they went.

Propagandists for the American empire have for some time presented Lincoln as an abolitionist. He was not. He disliked slavery but thought the federal government had no right to free other people's property—in this case, three million African-Americans at the South.

The Civil War was fought to preserve the Union, and, in the process, transformed it. Lincoln found that the bronze thread so idly woven into the Constitution provided him, as commander-in-chief, with the powers of a dictator. So he became dictator. He levied troops without consulting Congress, shut down newspapers, suspended habeas corpus, defied the Supreme Court—all in the name of "military necessity."

When the Supreme Court hurled the Constitution at Lincoln's head, Lincoln said he could do no other, as he had sworn an oath, "registered in heaven, to preserve, protect and defend the Constitution." The people agreed with their temporary dictator. And they reelected him in 1864.

The four-year war killed most of a generation of young men. Old Europe was astonished at the extent and ingenuity of this war and the novelty of its weapons—long-range artillery, ironclad ships. Bismarck sent observers. Then everybody sent observers.

Finally it became total war, which involved the civilian population to an unprecedented degree. Whole cities were deliberately burned to the ground. The South ran out of men and money, and collapsed. The Union had been preserved.

Lincoln's ambition

A recent biography makes much of Lincoln's remark, "I have not shaped events; events have shaped me." This gives us a new, passive Lincoln, a wealthy railroad lawyer suddenly made inept commander-in-chief in the first great modern war.

Of course, events control everyone, including imperial presidents. But at the center of Lincoln there is an ambition that is unlike that of any of his fellows. Also unlike them, he reveals himself at the age of 29 in a speech—a soliloquy—at Springfield, Illinois.

First he speaks of the founding fathers with polite admiration. "But," he says (always the *but*):

new reapers will arise, and they, too, will
seek a field...and when they do...the
question then is can that gratification be
found in supporting and maintaining an
edifice that has been erected by others?
Most certainly it cannot.

Thus Lincoln warns us against Lincoln.

Many great and good men...would
aspire to nothing beyond...the presidential chair; but such belong not to the
family of the lion or the tribe of the
eagle. What! Think you these places
would satisfy an Alexander, a Caesar or a
Napoleon?

Never! Towering genius disdains a
beaten path. It seeks regions hitherto
unexplored....It thirsts and burns for dis-
tinction, and, if possible, it will have it,
whether at the expense of emancipating
slaves or enslaving free men.

This "towering genius" recreated a nation
in his own marble image. Then, at the
moment of victory, comes the greatest
stroke of luck—he is murdered. Martyred.
And now, validated in blood, our Caesar
has become our god—and a loose confeder-
ation of states has become a sternly cen-
tralized federal system with a formidable
military capacity.

HIGH NOON

The mischievous press sometimes asks me, "Would you like to have been president?" And I say, "Well, politics is a family trade—yes."

But I was born a writer, and a writer must always tell the truth (unless he's a journalist), while the politician must never give the game away. In the end, it is better to have had some influence as a writer than to have bought—or have let someone buy for you—a title.

Projection of image and sound-bite slogans based on the latest polls is all there is to politics now. In the end, I was too interested in politics—and history—to take seriously election in the TV age.

On the other hand, I did sigh a bit when a cousin of mine became president. Of course, I lack Jimmy Carter's powerful vision and radiant charisma. Nor have I ever had the courage, while paddling a boat, to fight off the attack of a giant rabbit.

Jimmy Carter, 1977–1981

Today another cousin, "Al" Gore Jr., flits across the TV screens—a vice president lusting for promotion. At the school we went to, the boys nicknamed him Ozymandias, King of Kings. Should he ever achieve so boundless a wreck in the lone and level sands, I shall be Shelley.

Naturally, I do miss not having, if only for four years, my own TV studio in the White

House. That, as S.J. Perelman used to say, is the beauty part.

I did run twice for office. In 1960, as a candidate for Congress, I got 43% of the vote in my district, to Jack Kennedy's 38%. In 1964 the seat was mine if I wanted it, but by then I had gone back to novel-writing.

In 1982, I entered the California senatorial race, just to see what was going on. With hardly any money, I placed second in a field of four in the Democratic primary. And I also saw what was going on: He who spent the most money usually got the most votes.

Those senatorial candidates who did not have twenty or thirty million dollars of their own money to buy television ads were obliged to sell shares in themselves to the great conglomerates. In California, that meant the defense industries. As I was never keen on foreign wars, I was not what they had in mind for the Senate. Nor were they what I had in mind as employers.

Global emperors and dim presidents

The president's constitutional role as commander-in-chief allows him dictatorial powers if he can prove "military necessity." Lincoln's attachment to this phrase justified his wartime powers and also allowed him to emancipate the slaves, all in the name of military necessity.

29

Later presidents would take full advantage of Lincoln's free interpretation, because only in wars abroad could presidents free themselves of Congress and soar like eagles. Luckily for the generation after Lincoln, things were relatively quiet under a number of rather dim presidents.

In the late 1870s, Henry James came to Washington to stay with his friend Henry Adams, who decided to give a dinner party for the Master. James tells us that as Adams was drawing up his guest list, he became suddenly pensive. Then a deep breath.

"Why not be vulgar?" he said to James. "Let us invite the president."

So the dim Rutherford B. Hayes and his wife, known as Lemonade Lucy, entered high society. Actually, Hayes has a certain glamour in that his opponent, Samuel Tilden, was elected president by a quarter million votes in the centennial year 1876, and Congress and the Supreme Court, showing that they could be just as forcefully illegal as any president, reversed the election and the poignantly blameless Rutherford was thenceforward known as Ruther*fraud*.

The cross of gold

The dim presidents were eclipsed by the new breed of business millionaires. In the

Rutherford B. Hayes, 1877–1881

1870s, they diverted the nation with their exploits, much as Australian media moguls do today. They built their palaces along New York's Fifth Avenue and their seaside cottages at Newport, Rhode Island. Their monopolies came to dominate the economy, and the White House was little more than a branch office of "the firm."

But in the depressed South and West there was growing ferment among those who worked the land. Ruined by the Civil War, they were again being ruined by the financial games of Eastern banks. By 1896 America looked ready for a real class war.

Then out of the West came the greatest of American populist leaders, the radical William Jennings Bryan. Three times the Democrats nominated him for president, largely on the strength of his "Cross of Gold" speech:

> Burn down your cities and leave our farms and your cities will spring up again as if by magic. But destroy our farms and the grass will grow in the streets of every city of the country. You shall not press down upon the brow of labor this crown of thorns. You shall not crucify mankind upon a cross of gold.

The industrialists were terrified. The people were coming. But Bryan was narrowly defeated in the election of 1896 by the conservative William McKinley. Big Business had triumphed.

But the people at large were still so discontented that many leaders felt that an imperial distraction might prove useful. Why not put them in uniform? Why not conquer something?

The four horsemen

The British used to say that their empire was acquired in a fit of absent-mindedness. Ours was carefully thought out by four friends—the first time an empire has been actually planned. The reasons were mostly economic, as we shall see, but there was also a lot of derring-do.

Captain Mahan at the Naval War College was now applying his much-admired analysis of the British Empire to the United States. Essentially, he said, each was an island nation set on vast silver seas. To increase wealth, colonies were needed for raw materials and for markets.

Hence, build up a fleet which would need bases everywhere—thus acquiring, in the process, more colonies. So the more colonies, the more ships; the more ships, the more territories and markets—an irresistibly circular policy.

Henry Adams' brother Brooks was the first geopolitical thinker. He, too, lusted for empire; but his eyes were trained right across the Pacific. Brooks said that he who controls the wealth of Shanxi province in China will be master of the earth.

It was the job of Senator Henry Cabot Lodge and the bumptious assistant secretary of the Navy, Theodore Roosevelt, to implement the plan. But for this they needed a war, to get the whole thing started. During the summer of 1898, when President McKinley and the secretary of the Navy had left the capital for cooler climes, they set about finding one.

Britain was a possible enemy, but we might lose that one. Spain looked a safer bet, and its colonies included the Philippines, an ideal place from which to eye China—and, of course, closer to home, there were Cuba and Puerto Rico.

As if on cue, the US battleship Maine mysteriously blew up in Havana harbor. Whatever the actual cause, Spanish sabotage was blamed and the newspaper publisher William Randolph Hearst was able to unleash a tidal wave of anti-Spanish feeling.

Hearst claimed to have invented the war against Spain, but it was Roosevelt who really got things moving. As assistant secretary of the Navy, he ordered the US fleet to the Philippines during the government recess in the summer of 1898.

When the president returned to the capital, the Spanish fleet had been sunk and the Philippines seized with the aid of nationalist guerrillas, to whom we promised independence.

But McKinley decided we ought to keep the Philippines in order to Christianize the natives. When reminded that Filipinos were already Roman Catholic, the president responded, "Exactly." So we betrayed the nationalists and began our own conquest.

Unsurprisingly, reenactment films from the time chose not to dwell on the slaughter

William McKinley, 1897–1901

of some 200,000 men, women and children. But Mark Twain did salute our act of genocide by suggesting that we replace the stars and stripes in our flag with the skull and crossbones.

The president as busy seven-year-old

When McKinley was assassinated by an anarchist in Buffalo, Roosevelt, now the vice president, succeeded him. Roosevelt was our first international emperor. He was also the first president to dominate the mass media. The press corps accompanied him constantly. He was photographed and filmed everywhere, doing everything.

Roosevelt was in every sense a warrior emperor—a true apostle of war and a rhetorical precursor of Mussolini. "Speak softly, and carry a big stick," he said, as well as the interesting news that "no accomplishment of peace is half that of the glories of war."

And yet for his meddling in the Russian-Japanese conflict, he was awarded the Nobel Peace Prize. One must never underestimate Scandinavian wit.

Much has been made of TR's vigorous approach to, well, just about everything—charging around on horseback, a perilous expedition up the Amazon, the prodigious slaughter of wildlife on his innumerable safaris and hunting trips.

Henry Adams referred to him as our Dutch-American Napoleon. Henry James sighed, "He is the very embodiment of noise." The British ambassador was more kind. "We must never forget," he advised Whitehall, "that the president is seven years old."

Theodore Roosevelt, 1901–1909

It would seem that he was forever compensating for having been a sickly child, nearsighted and suffering from asthma. Give a sissy a gun and he'll shoot everything in sight.

Teddy regarded the presidency as a "bully pulpit." From the pulpit he attacked the scandalous rich while doing political business on the side with Standard Oil. He also believed it the Manifest Destiny of the white race to rule the degenerate coloreds.

His friend, Rudyard Kipling, wrote a poem for him urging him to take up "the white man's burden." And he did. TR's so-called "great white fleet" went on a goodwill cruise around the world.

Closer to home, TR realized a fifty-year-old American dream: a canal across Central America. When Colombia refused to give him the land, TR engineered a rebellion in the section he wanted, recognized the result as the new "free" Republic of Panama, and dug his ditch.

None of this, a member of his Cabinet noted admiringly, was in any way tainted by legality. Central America now had a new fun-loving friend to the north.

Big Business

TR's avatar, Woodrow Wilson, invaded
Mexico and Haiti—in order to bring those
poor people freedom and democracy and
good government. But stripped of all the
presidential rhetoric, the flag followed the
banks. The president was simply chief
enforcer for the great financial interests.
So, in one respect at least, the spirit of the
Constitution had been preserved.

Many years later, the commanding general of the US Marine Corps, General
Smedley Butler, blew, as it were, the whis-
tle, not just on Wilson, but on the whole
imperial racket:

> I spent most of my time being a high-class
> muscleman for Big Business, for Wall
> Street and for the bankers....In short, I was
> a racketeer, a gangster for capitalism....I
> helped make Mexico...safe for American
> oil interests in 1914...made Haiti and
> Cuba a decent place for the National City
> Bank boys to collect revenues in.

In later years, Butler also set up shop in
Nicaragua and the Dominican Republic, as
well as China, where in 1927 the Marines
protected Standard Oil's interests. In his
memoir, Butler grimly summed up his role:
"The best Al Capone had was three dis-
tricts. I operated on three continents."

Senator Gore and World War I

Woodrow Wilson had been a run-of-the-mill historian and an unpopular president of Princeton when he turned to politics. After only two years' experience as governor of New Jersey, he served eight years as president.

Woodrow Wilson, 1913–1921

Wilson was an eloquent, high-minded speaker who brought racial segregation to Washington. He wanted to be a domestic president, but his destiny lay elsewhere. As the Great War engulfed Europe, Wilson announced, "We are too proud to fight."

Actually, most of the nation was isolationist, while most of those who were interventionists preferred the kaiser to the British banks. This was inconvenient, as Wilson was not only an Anglophile but a good bank-man.

In 1916, my grandfather, Senator T.P. Gore, campaigned for Wilson's re-election on the ground that "he kept us out of war." But Wilson had other plans. He wanted war.

But first he had to get a declaration of war from Congress. This looked unlikely after his secretary of state, Bryan, resigned, in opposition to war.

When German U-boats threatened American shipping, Gore proposed a resolution forbidding Americans to travel the Atlantic. This was defeated.

Gore was as against meddling in foreign wars as I am. He knew, in this case, it was all for the sake of the banks, specifically J.P. Morgan. He reminded the country that the sacred Monroe Doctrine, which forbade

European governments the hectic joys and excitements of the Western Hemisphere, also denied us the fun and games of European wars.

He was to lose his seat in the Senate because he was against the First World War while, a generation later, his cousin, Senator Albert Gore Sr., lost his seat because he opposed the war in Vietnam. Albert Jr. broke with family tradition when he voted for the Bush-Ted Turner war in the Persian Gulf, and so became vice-president.

Predictably, U-boats sunk ships on which Americans were traveling, and Wilson promptly shredded the Monroe Doctrine. On April 2, 1917, he asked Congress for a declaration of war and got it. And oh, what a lovely war it was! (as the Joan Littlewood song goes).

I've often thought, had we stayed out, Germany might have dominated the European continent for a generation or so, and no one would have been the sadder. The kaiser was not Hitler. In fact, one suspects that a mildly victorious Germany in 1917 could never have produced a vengeful Führer fifteen years later.

But it wasn't to be. Troops were enlisted for the European war, and from that point on, we would be inextricably linked with Europe.

The Germans stopped fighting because Wilson had promised a peace without victory. But England and France had other plans—like revenge.

At Versailles, Wilson attempted to redraw the map of Europe. Blithely he erased the useful Austro-Hungarian Empire, replacing part of it with Yugoslavia, source of so much recent joy.

Wilson returned home thinking to be crowned with laurel, but Congress refused to ratify his new League of Nations. During a speaking tour, he was partially paralyzed by a stroke. But the administration continued with his wife, Edith, as regent, a constitutional mess no one knew how to handle.

FDR

After Wilson, we had no president of note until Franklin Roosevelt, who proved to be our Augustus. He was elected four times, a record.

He was a superb radio performer, and even better on film than his distant cousin Teddy. He called his newsreel performances, with characteristic modesty, "my Garbos."

Always seen looking hearty, he was in fact unable to walk due to polio. There was an unofficial agreement that no photographer show him with leg braces or in his wheelchair.

Franklin D. Roosevelt, 1933–1945

When he came to power in 1933, the country was deep in economic depression. Nature was also doing her bit by turning the best farmland into dust.

The New Deal was FDR's ramshackle plan to overcome the Depression. The government provided work for the unemployed. Many of our best public buildings were built in those days, and public education was at its peak. But recovery was fragile.

Ostensibly, like Wilson, Roosevelt set out to be a stay-at-home domestic president. But, unlike Wilson, he had inherited from his cousin Teddy a lust for foreign adventures.

Also, other empires were now loose in the world—the Germans in Europe and the Japanese in *our* Pacific. And then, despite the New Deal, the Depression flared up again in 1938. One-third of the work force was again unemployed.

FDR, hinting darkly of dangers from abroad, said we must rearm. He pumped $10 billion into the economy and ended the Depression in 1941. There was now full employment. Finally, without a declaration of war from Congress, FDR—both foe and ally of Big Business—waged his own presidential war against Germany, providing England with ships and arms. A newsreel of the time described our bullets as "steel-jacketed messengers of death from America to smash the Axis—another factor in the arsenal of democracy."

FDR thought this would be a replay of 1917. The Germans would sink our shipping and we would go to war.

Our ships were sunk. But not by the Germans. It was the Japanese, provoked by our sanctions and quarantining over their misdeeds in China and Manchuria, who sank much of our fleet at Pearl Harbor. Congress declared war, on December 8, 1941. This was to be the last time that Congress would be allowed to declare war.

Yalta

We arrived a bit late to the European conflict, but in perfect time to control the subsequent peace. Although our emperor was dying, he made his way to Russia—to Yalta, to meet with Churchill and Stalin.

At Yalta the world was carved up into spheres of influence. Stalin, fearful of yet another invasion from the west, held on to the states of eastern Europe as a buffer. It was agreed by all that Germany never again be rearmed.

Churchill looked upon FDR as friend and inseparable ally. But emperors can be neither. FDR coldly commanded the former colonial powers of England, France, Holland, to give up their empires—or else. As they were too poor to do otherwise, they let go.

As bits of the European colonial system came unstuck, they adhered like metal filings to the American magnet. There can be room for only one empire in the American world.

FDR condescended to what he called "Uncle Joe" Stalin, was sympathetic to his fears, let him have whatever it was he had taken—and nothing else. The Russian bear was then locked in his wintry cage, and FDR blithely pocketed the key.

To this day, right-wingers go on about how FDR sold us out at Yalta. Well, Stalin did get Romania. But we got West Germany. Stalin got some Japanese islands. We got Japan.

Some of the imperial presidents were sleepwalkers, like Jefferson when he bought Louisiana, or Woodrow Wilson when he was maneuvered by the bankers—and by his British friends—into the First World War. Other presidents, like Jackson and Polk, were aggressive land-grabbers, but only on our own continent. The Four Horsemen added the Pacific Ocean to our Western Hemisphere, and then, under Franklin Roosevelt, the entire significant globe, except for Russia and China, was ours.

In order to "contain" the new evil of Communism, we circled the globe with nuclear bases. We were home free at last. Well, fairly free. And not for very long.

TWILIGHT

Someone—Gibbon?—observed that as empires decline, they indulge in greater pageantry and show and—bluff. At Byzantium's end, the court rituals were so awesome and intricate as to paralyze the emperor.

American presidents are less showy. But I recall, as a boy, how easy it was to wander into the White House with only a few guards on hand. Now there are Secret Service men and armored cars, so that the embodiment of the nation can be seen but not shot.

Our presidents, now prisoners of security, have been for a generation two-dimensional figures on a screen—in a sense, captives of the empire they created. Essentially, they are men hired to give the commercials for a state which more and more resembles a conglomerate like General Electric.

In fact, one of our most popular recent presidents spent nearly twenty years actually doing commercials for General Electric, one of our greatest makers of weapons. Then Mr. Reagan came to work in the White House

television studio and there was the same
"Russians are coming" dialogue on the same
TelePrompTer, the same make-up men.

No president since Woodrow Wilson, who
left office in 1921, has written his own
speeches. The president reads what others
write. Sometimes he agrees. Sometimes
not. Sometimes he pays no attention.

Eisenhower always read his speeches
with a sense of real discovery. During his
first campaign for election, the country
was as excited as he when, in the middle
of his speech, he said, "And if elected, I
will go to—*Korea?*"

There was real fury in that reading. No
one had told him about that pledge. But go
to Korea he did.

In the event of nuclear attack, the president can speak directly to the military and
give codes for retaliation through the so-
called "football" that follows him wherever
he goes. There is a lot of advanced technology in the White House.

When Carter first sat at his desk in the
Oval Office, he was solemnly assured that
if he touched a certain button, a helicopter
would promptly arrive to remove him—and
the football—to safety. Carter pressed the
button. Presumably he is still waiting to be
rescued in Plains, Georgia.

Currently, as planes crash into Clinton's White House, and machine gun bullets spray the facade, the whole area has been cordoned off to keep our happy citizens at bay. The Secret Service was only partly joking when they recently told the Clintons that they would be happier if the president lived in a bunker and traveled through the streets of Persepolis in a tank.

Decline

The second law of thermodynamics assures us that everything is running down, and so the United States is no exception. But at the end of the Second World War we were on top of the world. And if anyone had told me then that so much would be acquired and lost in my lifetime, I would not have believed them.

But lose it we have. With hindsight I can now see that our ending was implicit all along. And the blame can be laid largely at one man's door: Eisenhower's predecessor, Harry S Truman (S for nothing).

Little was known in 1945 about the new president, other than that he played piano. Currently he is being turned into a hero, a Frank Capra sort of leading man who stands up for the little guy. Actually, he was a capable, sharp, machine politician who privately remained deeply unsure of himself in the big league.

When he took charge, a decision had to be made: to convert from war to peace or to maintain our military capacity at full strength. The economic reasons for maintaining a war economy were seductive, for president and arms manufacturers alike.

Harry Truman, 1945–53

The Democrat Truman was told by Republican Senator Arthur Vandenberg, *You're going to have to scare the hell out of the American people to make them spend all that money on war in peacetime.* Truman accepted the assignment.

The red menace

Truman set out to convince the American people that the Soviet Union meant to conquer the earth. The fact that we alone had the atomic bomb as well as bases all around the globe apparently counted for nothing. The fact that they had lost twenty million people was not factored in.

They were monolithic, and worse, Communism, always identified as godless *and* atheistic, was an attractive religion for evil people in every land, particularly in western Europe, where Communist and socialist and labor parties—they were all the same to Truman—were showing their postwar muscle. From the White House television studio, you can convince the whole world that black is white, up is down, freedom is slavery.

For nearly fifty years, occupants of the White House television studio have been able to convince most Americans that the Soviet Union was far in advance of us militarily and economically, even though a walk down a Moscow street was quite enough to convince even the most fearful anti-Red that Russia was a sad Second World country. The flush toilet was a mystery to them, while a workable top for a vodka bottle was the unattainable holy grail.

In due course they did become a formidable atomic military power of course. We had turned them into one.

The national security state

Truman was reelected—barely—in 1948. And we lost the opportunity of transforming our superpower status into prosperity and growth at home. By now the presidency had embraced the military and we were ready to become a national security state.

What is the national security state? Well, it began with the National Security Act of 1947 and was implemented three years later by a harmless-looking document known as National Security Council Directive No. 68, kept secret until the mid-1970s.

This contained the blueprint for a new kind of country, unlike anything the US had ever known before. First, there was to be a permanent Cold War. We would never negotiate—ever—with Russia.

Second, full speed ahead on developing the hydrogen bomb, so when the Soviets finally managed an atom bomb, we still wouldn't have to deal with them.

Third, rapidly build up conventional forces. Although Stalin had cut his military forces from twelve million to four million, a complete military draft was introduced—something unheard of in peacetime America.

Fourth, a massive increase in taxes to pay for all this. The sky's the limit, income tax as high as 90%.

Fifth, set up a strong alliance system of friendly nations, directed by the US. This was to become NATO, which tied western Europe to America militarily, effectively giving us dominion over a fourth continent. (When the first B29s landed in Britain in 1948, it was the first successful conquest of those islands since 1066.)

We could control and intimidate our allies with something called the CIA, with its secret, unconstitutional budget, and its mandate to overthrow governments, kill foreign leaders, do whatever dirty work needed doing.

And finally, mobilize the whole of America to fight the terrible specter of Communism. Root out the enemy within with lists of dissident organizations, wiretaps and surveillance—and loyalty oaths for all federal employees.

The first big adventure of the national security state occurred when South Korea was invaded by the Communist North. The generals and the CIA persuaded Truman that Moscow was challenging us in Asia. But since Truman did not dare ask Congress for an actual declaration of war, he settled for something called a United Nations police action.

In 1952, Truman was replaced by General Eisenhower, who went, as promised, to Korea. We were now locked into a land war in Asia.

Eisenhower

Two millennia and four centuries ago, Pericles observed that whether or not the Athenian empire had been obtained in good faith, once acquired, an empire is a very dangerous thing to let go.

With an American defeat on Asia's mainland—and Korea was a defeat—it was clearly time to start letting go those parts of the empire that were too expensive to maintain, using the money saved to spend at home for something eccentric, like schools. But the imperial momentum, institutionalized by Truman, was out of control.

Under Eisenhower, we replaced a popular leader in Iran, Mohammed Mossadegh, with the ill-fated Shah. Next a freely elected government in Guatemala was overthrown by the CIA. We interfered with governments on every continent, including Australia.

Dwight Eisenhower, 1953–1961

Yet Eisenhower was perhaps the only postwar president not to be hoodwinked by the military. He *was* the military. He understood their games. But that didn't make him soft on Communism.

When North Vietnam's new freely elected leader, Ho Chi Minh, a former chef at the Ritz Hotel in Paris, asked the United States to take Vietnam under its eagle wing to protect it from China, Eisenhower, in effect, told him: *You are a Communist. You're in league with the Chinese.*

In Eisenhower's memoirs, he is candid. Although the 1954 settlement at Geneva (to which we acquiesced but did not sign) guaranteed elections in 1956 for both north and south Indochina, it was plain that the northern Ho Chi Minh would win a free election.

Eisenhower duly noted that we could not allow that. And we did not. And so a long war began.

Eisenhower made the same gaffe with Castro. He hated Castro's beard and his uniform and his populist rhetoric and refused to meet him. Another *Communist.* Whatever Castro may or may not have been at the time, he certainly ended up in the arms of the Russians.

It wasn't until Eisenhower's farewell speech that he warned us that we were in danger of becoming a totally militarized economy:

> The total influence, economic, political, even spiritual, is felt in every city, every statehouse, every office of the federal government. We recognize the imperative need for this development, yet we must not fail to comprehend its grave implications. In the councils of government, we must guard against the acquisition of unwarranted influence, whether sought or unsought, by the military-industrial complex.

JFK

But incoming President John F. Kennedy wasn't listening: "Let every other power know that this hemisphere intends to remain the master of its own house." Kennedy made much of the fact that he was the first president to be born in this century—not much of an endorsement when one considers how terrible, in every sense, our century has been.

Kennedy was different from his predecessors, the cynical old presidents Truman and Eisenhower. They knew that the Communist threat was all nonsense. They also knew that it was good for business. But Kennedy believed the nonsense, and

John F. Kennedy, 1961–1963

he wanted to win the Cold War with a hot war somewhere or other.

Oddly for one so young, he spoke obsessively of "this twilight time." But then he was the first of our continuing line of twilight presidents. The noon now is gone for good.

Both Wilson and Franklin Roosevelt expected to be domestic presidents. And each became, more or less gladly, a war president. Kennedy was the reverse—he *wanted* to be a war president. "Who would ever have heard of Lincoln?" he once asked me, "without the Civil War?"

Although Jack was no Lincoln, he was easily one of the most charming men I've ever known. He was also, in retrospect, one of the very worst of our presidents.

He gave the green light to an invasion of Cuba and suffered a humiliating defeat. Nevertheless he was still so confrontational that Khrushchev, another geopolitical genius, put nuclear missiles into Cuba, bringing the whole world to that famous brink.

Then, undaunted, Jack started his hot war in Vietnam, by committing some 20,000 troops as advisers to the South Vietnamese Army.

The Vietnam War

In the gospel according to Oliver Stone, after a little trip to Dallas, Kennedy would bring back the troops that he had only just sent into battle. Why? Because he's the good guy.

Actually he had no intention of ending the war that he had just begun. "After Cuba," he told mutual friends, "I have to go all the way with this one."

Starting in 1964, I used to go on television and debate what seemed to be the entire American establishment. I did this for eight years. I thought the war was perfect folly. And I used to ask the president's advisers, on air, "What is this war about? Why are we in Vietnam?"

At first they said, *To contain China, forever on the march.* When I pointed out that the Vietnamese and the Chinese were ancient enemies, the subject would mysteriously change.

It is often remarked in the First World that, from the president on down, Americans are the most ignorant—in the literal sense of not-knowing what they ought to know—of any people with First World advantages.

My friends on the left were convinced that oil had been discovered in Vietnam and that we wanted it. I said that no one in our government had anything so reasonable as theft in mind. This was a war about vanity—imperial, presidential vanity.

We had been challenged by a small nation far, far from our shores and of no national interest to us. But to maintain our Wizard of Oz reputation as master of the planet, we had to destroy Vietnam in order to preserve it for democracy and freedom and, yes, the pursuit of happiness.

The war filled up our cemeteries, emptied our treasury of five trillion dollars, and defines us to this day. I don't know of any example in the history of the world—what little we can ever know of so shadowy a subject—where a country has done something so suicidal for no motive.

Finally, some twenty years after Eisenhower kept the people of Indochina from holding a national election because the "Communists" would have won it, the "Communists" drove us out of Vietnam, and our helicopters fled from the roof of the American Embassy compound in Saigon.

The destruction of LBJ

The war not only destroyed millions of lives and once-prosperous countries like Cambodia, it also destroyed a useful politician called Lyndon B. Johnson. Unlike the presidents we have been dealing with, he was not an imperialist. He wanted to complete the New Deal of Franklin Roosevelt. Do something for the people. Overcome race prejudice. Rebuild the US.

In the immediate wake of the Kennedy murder, he was able to get through an astonishing amount of domestic legislation, astonishing because the war-time Congress was now almost entirely repre-

THE DESTRUCTION OF LBJ

sentative not of the people but the great
corporations that profited from the war
while paying for national elections, as well
as for the media that tells us what to think
about public issues.

Johnson was undone by Kennedy's team
of academic hawks, the brothers Bundy
and the brothers Rostow, whom he had
fatally kept on, as well as the quintessen-

Lyndon Johnson, 1963–1969

tial corporate man, Secretary of Defense Robert McNamara, who recently confessed that he never really understood what the war was about.

Ironically, recently revealed tapes of Johnson's conversations during his early days in office show that he was perfectly aware that the war was unwinnable—and pointless—but he wasn't going to be "the first American president ever to lose a war."

Although he had been overwhelmingly elected as "the peace candidate" in 1964 against "the war candidate" Barry Goldwater, by 1968 the war was so unpopular that Johnson could make few public appearances outside military installations. Sadly, he chose not to run again, causing the Democratic party to split and thus ensuring the election of Richard Milhous Nixon.

Nixon

The supreme opportunist, he would do anything to get elected. "I pledge to you we shall have an honorable end to the war in Vietnam," he said. But Nixon had no plan and the war went on. As the nation was running down, the only glory point left was the space program.

It was launched under Kennedy, but Nixon got the good of it: "Hello, Neil and

Buzz, I'm talking to you by telephone from the Oval Room at the White House, and this certainly has to be the most historic telephone call ever made from the White House."

Why was he so pleased with himself? Well, Teddy Kennedy had just gone off the bridge at Chappaquidick, so Nixon's chief political rival was out of the picture and reelection was a certainty.

Richard Nixon, 1969–1974

After years of confrontation with China, Nixon paid a call on Chairman Mao. While Nixon was praising the Great Wall ("quite a wall"), he and Kissinger were bombing the independent countries of Laos and Cambodia in order, mysteriously, to break the unbreakable Viet Cong. This last futile exercise in genocide was called "linkage."

Then, in 1974, Nixon gave us his grand finale: for various civilian crimes committed in the election campaign of 1972, he resigned, the first president ever to do so. The next year the Vietnam war finally ended, and with it the dream of an all-American globe.

The Empire runs out of gas

Eleven years later, September 16, 1985, the Commerce Department finally announced that the US had become a debtor nation—in debt largely to our province, now creditor, Japan. At this point, the expanding American Empire came to a halt.

Four years later, when our mirror image and necessary enemy, the Soviet, decided to fold, it became clear that ultimately our status depended not on military prowess or a zeal to set up "democratic" regimes around the globe (a curious impulse on our part, since we were never that keen to try one at home), but on the so-called "money power" that had shifted from London to New York in 1914, and from New York to Tokyo in 1985. But then, for nearly half a century, perhaps two-thirds of the government's revenues had been siphoned to pay for what is euphemistically called "defense."[*]

---

[*]Government figures are, of course, faked from the start by including Social Security payments and disbursements as income and outgo. They are not. Social Security is an independent, slightly profitable, income-transferring trust fund, and should never be counted as federal revenue or federal spending. Here is the 1986 budget, a year after the dire news:

Gross federal revenue	$794 billion
Less Social Security contributions	294
Actual federal revenue	$500 billion
Defense	286
Foreign arms	12
Nuclear weapons (Energy Dep't.)	8
Veterans' benefits	27
Interest on past arms and wars	142
Total war spending	$475 billion

Thus fully 95% of revenues were allocated to war that year. Other federal spending was about equal to the deficit ($177 billion). Personal income taxes paid were only $358 billion. Therefore *all* of our US income tax was not enough to pay for the guns and ammo.

As the Asiatic colossus takes its turn as world leader, temporarily standing in for China, America becomes "the yellow man's burden." And so we come full circle. Europe began as the relatively empty, uncivilized Wild West of Asia. Then the Americas became the Wild West of Europe.

Now the sun, setting in our West, is rising once more in the East.

The three horsemen of the dusk

The collective dimness of Reagan, Bush and Clinton have proven to be something of a relief after the hectic fireworks of our great Augustus, Franklin Roosevelt, who imposed an American peace on the world while his heir, Harry Truman, like Augustus's heir, Tiberius, was the "chief founder of the imperial system in the lands of Europe"—and, despite a disaster in Korea, upon the eastern rim of Asia too.

Truman also resembled Tiberius because it was in the reign of each that "prosecutions for treason on slight pretexts first became rife, and the hateful race of informers was first allowed to fatten."[*]

---

[*] *Encyclopedia Britannica,* 11th edition.

Remember those 1950's loyalty oaths, blacklists, ruined careers due to FBI informers at home and to the newly created secret CIA agents busily at work in our far-flung provinces of Europe, Asia, Africa, Latin America, while at home there were cold-blooded show trials and even executions like that of Mr. and Mrs. Rosenberg, alleged spies for Parthia—I mean the Soviet—which took place later under General Vespasian...that is, General Eisenhower, whose heir, Kennedy....

Well, unlike Titus, Kennedy did not sack Jerusalem, but he did set in motion the Southeast Asian wars that were continued by his successors, Johnson and Nixon, on a scale that even the maddest of Roman emperors might have envied.

At the end, of course, we had to flee, thanks to the congenital weakness of the American people, who can usually be counted on to let down their selfless Caesars who had gone to all the trouble to use napalm and Agent Orange in order to make of Vietnam a wilderness in which they might proudly declare peace.

I shall strain no more the Roman analogy. We never really made it up to their league. The Roman empire lasted a half millennium, more or less successfully, while after a mere two centuries we are showing signs of wear and tear, particularly the Tiberius-Truman imperial system with its single all-powerful currency, the dollar, now challenged by the European Union and the ever more expensive, and pointless, NATO-ASEAN alliances.

Reagan and Bush

With Reagan, the Roman comparison well and truly ends. Of course he himself had fattened as an agent of the hateful race of informers, spying for the FBI on fellow Hollywood-persons who might be tainted with Communism.

But someone had to do it, so why not Ron? Rome, however, at its most decadent, had never thought of hiring an actor to go through the motions of being an emperor while the Praetorian Guard ruled.

With Reagan, the phantom Communism began seriously to drain off the Treasury's money. But he presided over a huge military buildup, and over the big taxes to pay for it. The actor's fans like to say that that is what drove the Russians out of business.

But they were falling apart quite on their own, while the buildup which was to lead us to Star Wars very nearly put *us* out of business. Even so, the Reagan mirage on that hill was a euphoric time for the few who make money out of "defense."

Finally, in a flurry of law-breaking (recycling enemy Iranian money from arms' sales to aid Nicaraguan rebels), Reagan went happily home to one of the many residences that his fans have always provided for him, gratis.

Ronald Reagan, 1981–1989

71

When I asked Katherine Graham, owner of the *Washington Post*, why her brave journal had not demanded Reagan's impeachment over "Iran Contra," a criminal conspiracy quite as mischievous as Nixon's dark plottings, she said, "Oh, we couldn't go through all that again just fourteen years later." Watchman, what of the night? The moon is down.

Contrary to rumor, George Bush did not put his wife Barbara's face on the one-dollar bill—that is still George Washington's green bewigged head, not savvy Barbara's. But Bush had his agenda: keep the empire going by constantly searching for very small enemies anywhere and everywhere while, at regular intervals, crying out piteously for a reduction of the capital gains tax, a matter of urgency to the 1% that own most of the country's wealth, but of no concern to the people at large—of whom over half no longer bother to vote, while lobbyists and their employers are thrilled at the even smaller turnout for other federal offices.

Of course, the media flourishes on the hundreds of millions of dollars that must still be spent at election-time for television ads which carefully steer clear of anything political, like health care, while indulging in ever more daring character assassination. Pedophiles now face off necrophiles. Toss a coin.

George Bush, 1989–1993

Reagan's most popular moment was when he smashed the Air Traffic Controllers' Union, thus making air travel less safe. Needless to say, Washington's National

Airport is to be renamed for him, the kind of fun that Caligula might have reveled in.

Envious of Reagan's victory over the very small island of Grenada, Bush found an enemy in little Panama, which he proceeded to bomb and invade. Then, after killing a number of Panamanians, he kidnapped their leader, Noriega, a long-time employee of the CIA, and proceeded to try him in a US court that had no jurisdiction over him, and found him guilty of charges that were vague to say the least, and locked him up.

All this was reminiscent of Stalin's heady reign, but then the United States has long since ceased to acknowledge international law of any kind. When summoned to the Court at The Hague for our crimes against Nicaragua, we refused to accept the jurisdiction of the international court that we had helped create.

Earlier, for equally idle reasons, Reagan ordered the bombing of another of our Enemy of the Month Club, Ghadaffi, because Libyans may have had something to do with a bomb that once went off in a German nightclub. As it turned out, they had no connection with the bomb in question but *our* bombs, intended to murder Ghadaffi, did succeed in killing his daughter—a proud day for the US of A.

After the great victory in Panama, Bush was ready for something really grand in the war line. A *safe* war, that is. The subsequent light-show in the Persian Gulf, as we have already noted, was great bread and circuses, and if Caligula had had television he might-just-have staged an even livelier Roman Scandals.

Bush enjoyed great instant popularity as a result of this uncalled for—and expensive—intervention. Newly demonized, like Noriega, Saddam had also been a CIA employee and his victim, Kuwait, was hardly a respectable "democracy."

Anyway, Bush's high proved to be fool's gold. A flattening economy put jobs at risk. A few people seemed to have all the money while 80% had nothing more than what working husband and working wife could make—which is less, as the famed statistic now goes, than what the husband alone made in 1973. So the hero from Kennebunkport, Texas was sent home while the man from Hope, Arkansas was duly installed in the White House.

The Clintons

As I write, President and Mrs. Clinton are under siege by what Hillary Clinton calls a right-wing conspiracy. Actually, the "conspiracies" (there are several) are not so much right-wing, which would imply politics, as a curiously ill-advised war of the rich against everyone else in general and against, in particular, any politician who might want to divert tax money back to the people in the form, say, of health care.

The current attacks on the Clintons are simply warning strikes. Warnings to other politicians. Don't touch our wealth. Warnings duly noted.

Although the Clintons are intelligent lawyers from the moderately well-off middle class, they came to "power" with little knowledge of how the ruling class (into which Bush had been born) operates. Most of our imperial Caesars were either born-in-the-purple patricians like the two Roosevelts or led by the hand—even nose—by the patriciate class, much as the elegant secretary of state, Dean Acheson, guided the dazed Harry Truman.

But despite attendance at the Yale Law School, Vatican for the patriciate's would-be politicians and managers, the Clintons never seemed to have met, say, a Mellon—like Mr. Mellon Scaife, whose wealth has been used to finance a foundation dedicated, apparently, to the ruin not only of the

Clintons but of any other social meliorist that dares speak for the 80%.

Bill Clinton, 1993–

There are, of course, reasonably sane Mellons and Rockefellers, du Ponts and Pews whose families own most of corporate America and hire often bright and always obedient lower-class persons—or even foreign helots, like Kissinger—to work for them, often directly, in the family cartel, or indirectly by placing them in the Congress, on the judicial bench, or in the White House.

Once representative government had been replaced by the imperial system of 1950, the corporate ownership is the only power in the land and not accountable to any authority since, with empire, it has been so internationalized that there is now no place where it hangs its hat and calls home.

At first, the election of Clinton was hardly traumatic: a rerun of Jimmy Carter. Southern moderate. No surprises—or so the ownership concluded, shifting the Republican Candidate Dole from politics to sales, where he contentedly pitches American Express cards on TV. Or whatever.

It was assumed that the Clintons knew the rules of the game: Do nothing at home unless the banks give the green light and the boardrooms sign on. Foreign capers are allowed, but costs must be kept low. Stick to places like Panama, Grenada or the Persian Gulf. Keep Wolf Blitzer, Wolf Blinken, Wolf Nod baying happily on CNN. Makes money for advertisers. Sells newspapers.

Unfortunately, Clinton didn't get it. Or if he got it, then he lost it. He seemed to think that the president of the United States is a man of power who can rev up the economy and even do things that need doing for the people at large.

He seemed *not* to know that the office he holds is as powerless as it is expensive to gain, rather like elections to the Roman consulships, which were retained to the end of the empire while Caesars did the ruling. They kept the *forms* of an ancient and revered republic while depriving consuls and Senate of those powers to rule which were now the emperor's sole prerogative.

Thus far, corporate power has only twice allowed imperial powers to their president. In wartime, Lincoln and FDR were both imperial and tyrannical in their powers and the people, not to mention their economic masters, more or less willingly supported these temporary usurpations.

But in peacetime, as that clever scalawag Nixon used to observe, you don't really need a president. The place runs itself. Foreign affairs is what's interesting and, let's face it, domestic affairs are pretty boring. In Nixon's eagerness not to be bored, he allowed the "liberalism" of the New Deal to stumble along the Yellow Brick Road for a bit longer while he created havoc in Asia.

Clinton began with what appeared to be no interest in foreign affairs. On the other hand, he would give the people what every other prosperous First World nation had—a health service, paid out of taxes which had for so long been earmarked for "defense."

The campaign against health care

The war that the Clintons lost so famously to the ownership is a classic example of how the US is actually managed—but not, perhaps, as clear as it ought to be to a people who have been conditioned from birth to believe that Americans possess neither an empire nor a ruling class.

Even so, the point still got through to a great many of those who managed to withstand the overwhelming TV blitz against national health care:

Harry, does this health thing mean we can't use kindly Dr. Haskins who delivered our precious Buster Brown?

I'm afraid, Louise, that's just what this thing means.

But, Harry, that's common-ism.

That was also crude but masterful PR. What the Clintons had done was challenge those insurance companies that, under our present costly private system, collect around a third of what is spent on private health care, for which they give back not even a Band-Aid.

To be blunt, the insurance companies are the cash cow of the richest 1% of the population. They are also sort of piggy banks for international conglomerates like ITT who, in 1973, bought Hartford Life Insurance.

Methodically, the ownership has set out to destroy the Clintons. Since actual politics may not be discussed in freedom's land, the "crimes" of one's enemies are all that's left. The hapless couple were accused of murder, sexual perversions, larcenies both great and small as well as—the horror! the horror!—*ill grooming.*

Nothing personal, Bill, Hillary. Soon as you're out of office there's big bucks, and big jobs with your names on them, at any one of our enterprises. Meanwhile, we have to use you to send a message to all the other dummies out there:

Don't mess with us. It's our country, not yours. We paid for it. We're not selling. And forget about taxing us. Anyway, isn't it pretty exciting now we got just about the whole globe?

Soon we'll get into China. Big market. Cheaper than going to war with them but maybe we'll have to go that route too, one of

these days. The big one. Meanwhile, just
keep government off our backs.

The war against the people

There is a chuckle at this one. Ever since
the Supreme Court interpreted the 14th
Amendment to mean the application of the
Bill of Rights to corporations as well as to
"persons" within the states of the United
States, there has been one law for the
lion...but let us quote the great conservative, E. Burke: "People crushed by law have
no hopes but from power. If laws are their
enemies, they will be enemies to laws."
Enter Reno of Waco.

Although external war has been the tra-
ditional means of extending our empire,
new technology has made the ultimate war
of rich against poor highly tempting and,
perhaps, even winnable, as the state,
instead of withering away, flourishes like
algae in sewage.

For instance, the arbitrary and pointless
prohibition of drugs has led to an internal
"war" by the government against the "persons" who live under their ever stricter
control. They have locked up a couple of
million persons more or less at random,
keep millions more under constant surveillance with mandatory blood, urine, lie-

detector tests, while TV cameras record our movements.

We can no longer turn to Clinton or to any politician who can be elected president under the present system. I am often asked by Europeans, *Why is there no left, no radical party, no labor party, no just plain representative-of-the-people-at-large party in the United States?*

The answer is simple. Our media is strictly controlled by interlocking corporations—oh, synergy. This means that if a great leader were to come along, would his speeches be reported in the *New York Times?* No. Would he get more than a sound bite on the evening news? No. Would Ted Koppel invite him on his rigged program? No.

But if, by chance, he were to acquire a popular following, like Jesse Jackson in 1988, he would be accused of something bizarre like anti-Semitism (anti-white might have been more to the point, and for good reason). No liberal voice is now allowed on prime-time television or the op-ed pages of a press so partisan that it is not even aware there is another side to its relentless celebration of the way things are. (By the way, I use the word *liberal* in the mildest old-fashioned sense of someone who would like to extend the democracy to include, one utopian day, those without money.)

Historical quibbles

The reflections on the imperial presidency in this little book actually did get shown as a television documentary—in the United Kingdom: three half-hour programs on Channel Four. Then the History Channel bought the program sight unseen for the US. When it *was* seen—panic. To cancel it would have been the wisest course. Instead, they opted for discrediting the program as it was shown.

The History Channel, though itself small potatoes, is owned, variously, by some of the world's most powerful corporations and opinion-makers. So the American showing of *Gore Vidal's American Presidency* would be presented by Disney-ABC television in conjunction with General Electric-NBC as well as the Hearst Corporation's Arts and Entertainment.

Since General Electric was responsible for many costly overruns at the Pentagon (not to mention the presidency of their long-time pitchman, Ronald Reagan), they solved the embarrassment of my commentary by using two TV journalists to remark, from time to time, that I was wrong about everything, because I hated America.

Then, at the end, two historians were trotted out to note the serious errors. As always, one was Arthur Schlesinger, flack for empire, who did admit that I probably didn't really hate America but was plainly "disappointed" in the way things had gone since 1950.

Then the quibbles began. Arthur said that I had misquoted the Declaration of Independence. Apparently, he hadn't realized that I was quoting from Jefferson's original draft, something most American historians recognize.

Since I was discussing imperial presidents, I noted that Polk gave us the Southwest, Oregon, California and Texas. Schlesinger said that Polk's successor Tyler acquired Texas. This is a peculiar quibble.

On March 1, 1845, Congress passed a joint resolution (of dubious legality) annexing Texas as well as what is now Oklahoma, New Mexico, Kansas and Colorado. Three days later, Tyler left office and Polk was inaugurated.

In December, Texas became the 29th state, under Polk. Mexico objected to all of this and so Polk went to war in order to gain the Southwest and California.

On February 2, 1848, Polk approved the treaty of Guadelupe-Hidalgo, wherein defeated Mexico ceded to the US all Texas to the Rio Grande, New Mexico and upper California. So it is fair to say Polk and not Tyler (nor Congress) annexed Texas. And so on.

Coda

We are supposed to be grateful for our freedom to write and say what we choose, while acknowledging humbly the media's freedom neither to print nor to record accurately—or at all—what we might say in disagreement to the boardroom's version of human events. Now the struggle is on for control, if such is possible, of the Internet and of space itself, both within and all round the human mind. That will be the great war.

Meanwhile, a sane polity would go back to Philadelphia, as Jefferson suggested we do once a generation, and replace an odious and dangerous empire with something like the original republic. But the 1% that matters and the 20% that is doing well working for them will not allow the rest of us to free ourselves so easily.

Opinion will be entirely against a constitutional convention. After all, as Herder observed, "The State is happiness for a group." Our little group is very, very happy indeed, and it will hold until....

As I ended the program, I meditated on Nixon's famous "silent majority"—not the fierce bigots that he had in mind but the dead—specifically those dead in our wars. The camera then showed Washington—a city crowded with funerary monuments, from Arlington cemetery to the Lincoln memorial.

All good things must end, I said to camera. Bad things too. As you must suspect by now, I am a lover of the old republic, and I deeply resent the empire our presidents put in its place. And I actively hate the national security state—now, let us hope, in its final days.

Let us hope that the last hurrah of Truman's legacy was the Gulf War. Iraq invaded freedom-loving Kuwait and we were told by CNN: "The skies over Baghdad have been illuminated." What a long way we have come since Thomas Jefferson's Declaration of Independence:

> We hold these truths to be sacred and undeniable: that all men are created equal and independent, that from that equal creation they derive rights inherent and inalienable, among which are the preservation of life, and liberty, and the pursuit of happiness.

And now, my home city of Washington has become nothing but a vast memorial to those dead in wars that have glorified the odd president, enriched the military-industrial complex, but left the rest of us—we the people, the nation—with this:

© 1995 Larry Powell

The Vietnam Veterans Memorial, Washington DC

INDEX

89

⇒ ⇒ IF YOU LIKED THIS BOOK,

WHAT UNCLE SAM REALLY WANTS
NOAM CHOMSKY

A brilliant look at the real motivations behind US
foreign policy, from the man the NY Times called
"arguably the most important intellectual alive."
111 pp. $8.50.   *Highly recommended. –Booklist*
140,000 copies in print worldwide

THE PROSPEROUS FEW
AND THE RESTLESS MANY   NOAM CHOMSKY

A wide-ranging state-of-the-world report that
covers everything from Bosnia to biotechnology.
Chomsky's fastest-selling book ever. 95 pp. $8.
Calmly reasoned. Most welcome. –Newsday
109,000 copies in print worldwide

SECRETS, LIES AND DEMOCRACY
NOAM CHOMSKY

This fascinating book explains how the Nazis
won WWII, why the US is becoming more like a
Third World country, and much else. 127 pp. $9.
80,000 copies in print worldwide

THE CHOMSKY TRILOGY

A boxed set of the three titles above. $24.

TAKE THE RICH OFF WELFARE
MARK ZEPEZAUER
& ARTHUR NAIMAN

How we spend at least $448 billion a year on
"wealthfare." 191 pp. $12.

A fascinating story everyone should read. –Gore Vidal
Concise and clear....a very useful tool. –Noam Chomsky
24,000 copies in print

CHECK OUT SOME OF OUR OTHERS:

THE COMMON GOOD   **NOAM CHOMSKY**
This illusion-shattering masterpiece discusses
Aristotle, the US left and everything in between.
191 pp. $12.   *Fall, 1998*

**THE DECLINE AND FALL
OF THE AMERICAN EMPIRE**   **GORE VIDAL**
This delightful book is the perfect introduction
to Vidal's witty political writing. 95 pp. $7.50.
     Deliciously, maliciously funny. –NYT Book Review
31,000 copies in print

THE CIA'S GREATEST HITS
     MARK ZEPEZAUER
The CIA's many attempts to assassinate
democracy are described in 42 brief chapters,
each accompanied by a cartoon. 95 pp. $7.
21,000 copies in print

EAST TIMOR: GENOCIDE IN PARADISE
     MATTHEW JARDINE
     INTRODUCTION BY NOAM CHOMSKY
Chomsky calls it "perhaps the greatest death toll
relative to the population since the Holocaust."
The US supports the genocide. 95 pp. $6.

---

*Real Story books should be available at any good book-
store, but if you can't find them there, you can also buy
them directly from Common Courage Press, Box 702,
Monroe ME 04951. Shipping within the US is $2.50 for
1 book, $3.50 for 2–4 books or $4.50 for 5–9 books.*

*For shipping costs for larger—or foreign—orders,
information on quantity discounts, or to order by credit
card, please fax 207 525 3068, call 207 525 0900 or
800 497 3207, e-mail odonian@realstory.com, visit
www.realstory.com or write us at the address above.*

The Real Story Series is based on a simple idea—
political books don't have to be boring. Short, well-written
and to the point, Real Story books are meant to be <u>read</u>.

Here are a few excerpts from this provocative book:

George Washington acquired much of his fortune in the
most honest way—he married it. The first president
was our first millionaire.

During his two terms, Andrew Jackson broke 93 treaties
with Indian tribes.

Lincoln became a dictator. He levied troops without
consulting Congress, shut down newspapers, suspended
habeas corpus, defied the Supreme Court—all in the name
of "military necessity."

Truman and Eisenhower knew the communist threat was
all nonsense. They also knew that it was good for business.
   But Kennedy believed the nonsense, and wanted to win
the Cold War with a hot war somewhere or other. "Who
would ever have heard of Lincoln," he once asked me,
"without the Civil War?'

The Clintons seemed to think that the president of the United
States is a man of power who can do things for the people
at large. They challenged the insurance companies that
collect a third of what is spent on private health care.
Methodically, the ownership has set out to destroy the

ISBN 1-878825-15-1
50800

9 781878 825155

$8

Odonian Press
distributed throug
Common Courag
Press / LPC Gro